People or Wildlife?

Terry Jennings
Photographs by Jenny Matthews
Illustrations by Peter Bull Art Studio

A & C Black · London

Contents

The world's wildlife 4
The biggest and smallest creatures, different
species, the wildlife around you

The balance of nature 6
How plants make food, food chains and food webs

Upsetting the balance 8
How people and wildlife are affected when a food
chain is disrupted, predators and prey

Why people need wildlife 10
How we depend on many animals for food, clothes
and medicines, why conservation is important; is it
wrong to eat meat?

Extinction 12
Why do creatures become extinct?

Hunting 14
Why people hunt animals, how hunting and
poaching have affected wildlife, what can be done
to prevent more creatures becoming extinct

Cover photographs
Front – Testing a pond for pollution (see pages 20–21)
Back – Performing Killer Whale (see pages 28–29)

Title page photograph – Keeping goats for food (see
page 10)
Acknowledgements
Photographs by Jenny Matthews except for: p.4
Robert Pickett, Papillio; p.7b Terry Jennings; p.9
Philip Marazzi, Papillio; p.10b Terry Jennings; p.11
Daniel Dancer, Still Pictures; p.13t J. Jackson/WWF
UK; p.13b Mark Edwards/Still Pictures; p.14 Jamie
Harron, Papillio; p.15t M. Rautkari/WWF; p.15b
Norbert Wu, Still Pictures; p.16t Robert Pickett,
Papillio; p.16b Mattias Klum/WWF UK; p.17, 22
Terry Jennings; p.231 Mark Carwardine, Biotica; p.24
Terry Jennings; p.25t F. Sullivan/WWF UK; p.25b
Mark Edwards, Still Pictures; p.26 and 27 Mark
Carwardine, Biotica; p.28 Dave Currey/WWF UK;
p.30t Laura Sivell, Papillio; p.31t Robert Pickett.

The author and publisher would like to thank the
following people for their invaluable help during the
preparation of this book: the staff and pupils of
Grasmere J.M.I. School and Bolshaw Primary School.

A CIP record for this book is available from the
British Library.

ISBN 0-7136-3543-6

Unpopular and too popular   16
How some creatures have become extinct because
people are afraid of them, how other animals are
under threat because people want them as pets but
cannot or do not look after them properly

Pollution   18
How wildlife is put in danger by people's activities;
wildlife as pollution indicators, how to stop pollution

Unwelcome guests   22
The disastrous consequences that can happen when
people introduce wildlife from one country into another

Habitat destruction   24
What happens when people destroy wildlife habitats
and what can be done to stop further destruction?

Protecting wildlife   26
Providing safe places for plants and animals to live
and breed, how game wardens protect wildlife

Wildlife and zoos   28
Why some people are in favour of zoos and why
others think that zoos are damaging to wildlife

Make a wildlife reserve   30
Making wildlife habitats at home or school

Useful addresses and index   32

First published 1992 A & C Black (Publishers) Ltd
35 Bedford Row, London WC1R 4JH

© 1992 A & C Black (Publishers) Ltd

Typeset by Rowland Phototypesetting Ltd,
Bury St Edmunds, Suffolk
Printed in Italy by Imago

The world's wildlife

There are over a million different kinds of animal living in the world today. They range in size from the Blue Whale, which can grow to be more than 30 metres long, to animals so tiny you could fit hundreds of them on to a pin head.

Scientists arrange all living things into species. A species is a group of animals or plants which is different from all the other groups. Today there are about 4500 species of mammal (of which humans are one species) and around 700,000 species of insect.

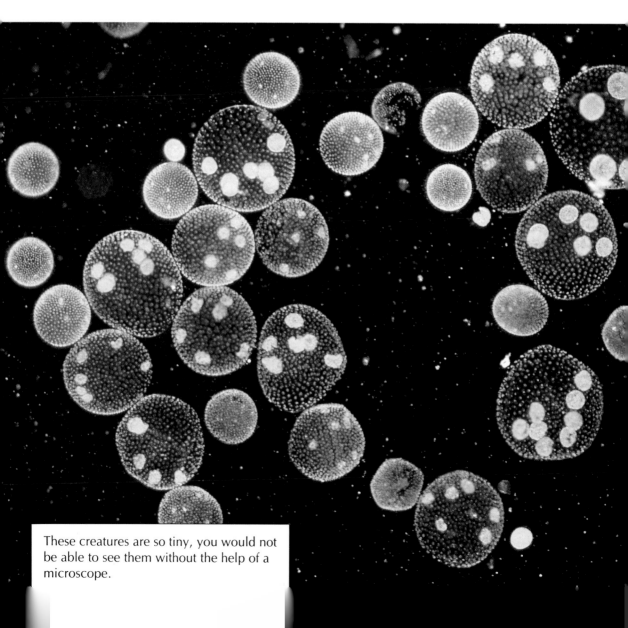

These creatures are so tiny, you would not be able to see them without the help of a microscope.

Study your local wildlife

Even quite a small patch of ground provides a home for hundreds of different species of animal, although you'll need a magnifying glass to see most of them.

1 Look for wildlife around your garden, a local park (make sure you get permission first), or a piece of waste ground. Look under logs, pieces of wood, stones and in cracks in the bark of trees. Use a magnifying glass to help you see the smaller creatures more clearly.

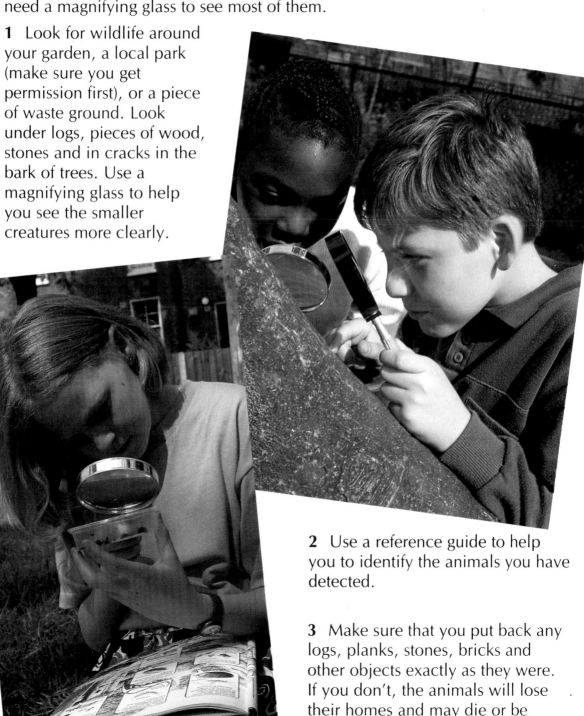

2 Use a reference guide to help you to identify the animals you have detected.

3 Make sure that you put back any logs, planks, stones, bricks and other objects exactly as they were. If you don't, the animals will lose their homes and may die or be killed.

The balance of nature

Without food, living things die. Plants make their own food using sunshine, water, and carbon dioxide from the air. They are the only living things which are able to do this, so all animals depend on plants for food.

Even meat-eaters or carnivores depend on plants, because they eat plant-eating animals called herbivores. The carnivores may themselves be eaten by bigger, fiercer carnivores. This chain of:

plant → herbivore → first carnivore → second carnivore is called a food chain.

Food chains are rarely as simple as, for example, grass → rabbit → fox because lots of animals eat grass besides rabbits, and lots of animals eat rabbits besides foxes. When several food chains become connected together, they make a food web. How many food chains are you part of?

A food chain

Plant e.g. lettuce
eaten by

Herbivore e.g. Garden Snail
eaten by

First carnivore e.g. Song Thrush
eaten by

Second carnivore e.g. Merlin

Study a food chain

Aphids (Greenfly or Blackfly) are tiny herbivores which feed on plant juices.

1 Find a plant such as a rose bush which has aphids feeding on it. Pick off a leafy shoot which *doesn't* have any aphids on it. Put the shoot in a small bottle of water and plug the gap around the top of the bottle with cotton wool.

2 Stand the shoot and bottle in a large jar. Using a paintbrush, carefully move one aphid from the bush on to the leafy shoot. Cover the top of the jar with some muslin or stocking material.

3 Watch the aphid carefully with a hand lens to see how it uses its pointed mouthparts to suck the juices from the plant.

Keep watching the aphid very closely. Before long it will give birth to a baby aphid. Make a regular count to see how many aphids there are in your jar.

4 After a day or two, put a ladybird in to the jar. Watch how it catches and eats the aphids. Write or draw a food chain for the ladybird and aphids.

Upsetting the balance

With so many food chains all linked together, it is not surprising that if something happens to one plant or animal, many more can be affected.

In some European countries, the legs of edible frogs are eaten in restaurants. There is a shortage of European frogs because many of the ponds and ditches where they live have been drained or polluted. At one time, someone thought it would be a good idea to catch the bullfrogs that live in the wet rice fields of India to sell to restaurants in Europe.

When the insect-eating frogs were removed from the rice fields, the insects were able to multiply until they were out of control. Before long the rice crop failed, attacked by swarms of insects.

The people who farm rice fields like this one, depend on a plentiful supply of predators to keep the numbers of insect pests under control.

The balance of nature in the rice fields had been upset, with the result that the people of India had to buy more expensive rice from other countries, or else go hungry.

A cheetah chasing its prey on the grassy plains of Africa has a better chance of catching an animal which is sickly or weak.

In the natural world, the numbers of plants and animals are delicately balanced. Carnivores, or predators, like ladybirds, bullfrogs and foxes, which catch and eat other animals, play an important part in controlling this balance.

As well as controlling populations, predators may actually improve the health of the species they prey on by weeding out sick and weak animals. Only the stronger and healthier animals are left to breed.

Why people need wildlife

When people damage their surroundings and upset the balance of nature, they are harming themselves and others, as well as the plants and animals that share our world.

All the food we eat comes from plants and animals. Plants also keep the air we breathe supplied with oxygen which they give out when they are making their food.

In many parts of the world, people keep animals for their meat, or milk.

We also depend on many species of animal for medicines and clothes. Are you wearing anything today such as a jumper or a pair of shoes that is made from part of an animal?

Some people think that we shouldn't eat meat. The animals that are bred for their meat are reared on farms which cover huge areas of land. Often forests are cleared to make way for this farmland, destroying the surroundings of many different species of wildlife.

▲ In the African savanna, Wild Buffaloes could be cross-bred with farm Buffaloes to produce strong, healthy animals. But it will soon be impossible for scientists to do this because the Wild Buffalo is now an endangered species.

Each year, nearly half the world's cereal crop is used as feed for farm animals. But only a small amount of this is turned into meat. The crop could have been used to feed many more people than can be fed by the meat from farm animals reared on the same amount of cereal. Plants and animals are important to us in lots of ways. But even if they weren't, don't you think they have as much right to be here as we do?

▼ 'Clear-cut' forest clearance in the United States has destroyed huge numbers of trees.

Extinction

Most of the millions of species of animals and plants that have ever lived have died out or become extinct. New species of animals and plants slowly develop, or evolve, to replace them. This process happens over thousands or even millions of years. It is called evolution.

▲ These are just some of the thousands of creatures which are currently threatened with extinction. The animals have not been drawn to the same scale.

Extinction is a normal part of evolution. In the past, species became extinct because of natural causes. Some, like the dinosaurs, may have died out when new species appeared which were better at finding food, or better suited to the conditions.

People have made many species become extinct. At one time there were more North American Passenger Pigeons than any other bird in the world. A naturalist who tried to count one large flock estimated that it was 240 miles long and contained two billion pigeons. Less than 100 years later, hunting had made the passenger pigeon almost extinct. The last one died in a zoo in September 1914.

◀ Whales such as the Blue Whale and the Humpback Whale are nearly extinct because, until recently, they were ruthlessly hunted for their meat, oil and bones. Most countries have now agreed to stop the killing, but it will be a long time before whales increase to anything like their former numbers.

Species are now becoming extinct 1000 times faster than they did before humans appeared on the Earth. Some scientists think that a million species are endangered and may become extinct by the year 2000 unless we do something to protect them. They include over 500 species of mammal and 1000 species of bird.

What you can do

We need to conserve as many different species of wild animals and plants as possible. You can help by joining groups who are campaigning for the protection of wildlife. There is a list of addresses to write to at the back of this book.

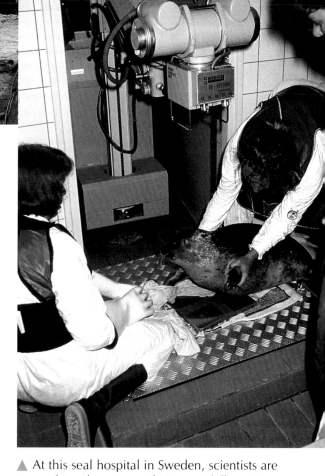

▲ At this seal hospital in Sweden, scientists are researching the causes of injury and illness in seals and are helping to restore sick seals to health.

Hunting

Stone Age people lived by hunting animals and gathering wild plants. They had to hunt for their food or they would starve. They only killed the animals they needed for themselves and their families to eat.

Nowadays, most people do not need to hunt, as their food is grown on farms. Hunting still goes on though, but today it is often to make money or simply for fun.

▲ This elephant was killed by poachers.

In 1979 there were about 1.3 million African Elephants. Thousands have been killed by illegal hunters called poachers. The poachers killed the elephants for their ivory tusks which were then made into expensive jewellery and ornaments. Now there are only about 600,000 elephants left.

▶ These ivory souvenirs were carved from elephants' tusks.

Tigers, leopards, cheetahs, ocelots and many other wild cats are very rare because they are hunted for their striped or spotted skins which are used to make fur coats. Many kinds of reptile such as crocodiles, alligators, lizards and snakes are killed and their skins made into handbags, shoes, wallets and belts.

Uncontrolled hunting for food can also make whole species extinct. Many species of food fish are becoming rare because they are being caught faster than they can breed.

To make matters worse, the fishing vessels often accidentally catch and kill dolphins and porpoises which get tangled up in their huge nets. These species have already become endangered by pollution.

◀ This Sea Lion is slowly being strangled by a fishing line which has become tangled around its neck.

What you can do:

✳ Buy cans of fish which have a 'dolphin-friendly' label. This means that the fish have been caught without causing harm to dolphins.

✳ If you go on holiday abroad, don't buy presents or souvenirs made from parts of animals.

Unpopular and too popular

Some animals have become extinct or rare because people do not like them or are afraid of them. For example, many people wrongly believe that wolves are dangerous to humans. Because of this fear, wolves were extinct in England by the reign of Henry VIII and the last wolf in Scotland was killed in 1743. Wolves are also now very rare or extinct over much of the rest of Europe.

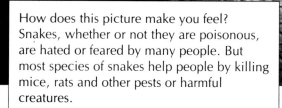

How does this picture make you feel? Snakes, whether or not they are poisonous, are hated or feared by many people. But most species of snakes help people by killing mice, rats and other pests or harmful creatures.

▲ This young Orang-utan has been captured and taken from the wild.

As a result, people all over Europe now have to keep the number of deer under control using guns. They are having to do the work the wolves used to do for them.

Some animals face extinction because they are too popular. Until recently, thousands of tortoises were dying each year. They were caught in their own countries, packed into crates and sent to Europe to be sold as pets. Many died on the way, while most of the rest died during their first winter in a colder land. The lives of birds such as parrots, macaws and cockatoos are still threatened in this way.

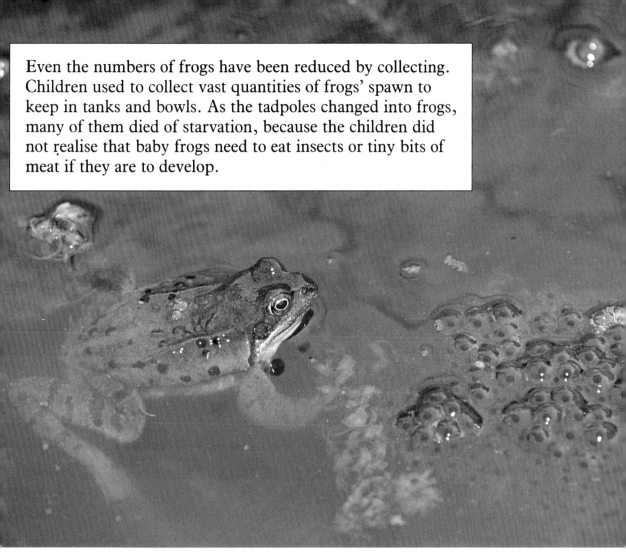

Even the numbers of frogs have been reduced by collecting. Children used to collect vast quantities of frogs' spawn to keep in tanks and bowls. As the tadpoles changed into frogs, many of them died of starvation, because the children did not realise that baby frogs need to eat insects or tiny bits of meat if they are to develop.

What you can do:

* Treat all animals, even those you don't like, with great care. If you don't like spiders, for example, and you see one indoors, ask someone to scoop it up and let it go outside or in a garage. Spiders are harmless creatures and they are good at keeping your home free of flies.

* If you buy a pet bird, make sure it has been bred in captivity and not imported from overseas.

* Do not have your photograph taken with monkeys, chimpanzees or any other exotic animals. These have probably been taken from the wild and they are often badly treated by their owners.

* If you collect frog or toad spawn, take only about a dozen eggs. Let the tadpoles go, in a suitable pond, when their legs begin to grow.

Pollution

▲ Sewage flows onto a beach in Italy. In some countries, beaches have been closed altogether because they have become so polluted by sewage.

Pollution is the dirtying of air, land or water with substances which would not normally be found there. Almost everything people use, from cars to washing powders, causes pollution either when it is being made or when it is used.

Sewage or natural waste can be treated by a process which makes it harmless. But in many countries, untreated sewage is dumped into rivers, lakes or seas where it kills water animals and plants.

Powerful chemicals are used on farms to kill pests, weeds and diseases. Unfortunately, these chemicals are often long-lasting, and they kill not only the pests they are intended for, but useful animals as well.

These chemicals are particularly dangerous when they build up in a food chain (look back at pages 6 and 7). When a big animal eats lots of smaller ones, which have eaten tiny quantities of poison, the larger animal may take so much poison into its body that it either dies or cannot breed.

▲ This forest in Sweden has been sprayed with lime in an attempt to fight the effect of acid rain. Lime is an alkali which is the chemical opposite of an acid. When an alkali is added to an acid, they cancel each other out, so that the resulting mixture is neither alkaline nor acidic.

▼ Crops on this farm in Italy are being sprayed with chemicals called pesticides.

Gases in the smoke from car exhausts and factory and power station chimneys mix with the air to form acids. These combine with water to form acid rain, which kills trees and pollutes lakes and rivers, poisoning fish and other animals.

As well as being ugly to look at, litter damages the environment and can be harmful to wildlife. Discarded cigarette ends and matches start fires. Empty bottles and cans trap and kill small animals. Plastic bags and cups, and the plastic rings from packs of drinks cans sometimes suffocate or choke animals.

Animals can provide us with a good indication of the levels of pollution in a certain area. In rivers, fish soon die when the water becomes polluted; so too do many much smaller animals such as Mayfly larvae.

How polluted is your local pond, river or stream?

1 Stand on the bank and study the water carefully. Is there any oil floating on the surface? You can tell by the rainbow patterns oil makes.

2 Carefully collect some of the water and hold it up to the light. Polluted water is sometimes cloudy.

3 Dip a net into the water and gently transfer any animals you catch into a white dish or tray. Look at them carefully. Some animals are very sensitive to pollution and can only live in the cleanest water. A few can live in quite dirty or polluted water.

▲ When people drop litter into a pond, they threaten the survival of many of the pond's creatures.

4 A reference guide will help you to identify any animals that you catch. Match up the names to the pictures on this chart. Then you can tell how polluted the water is.

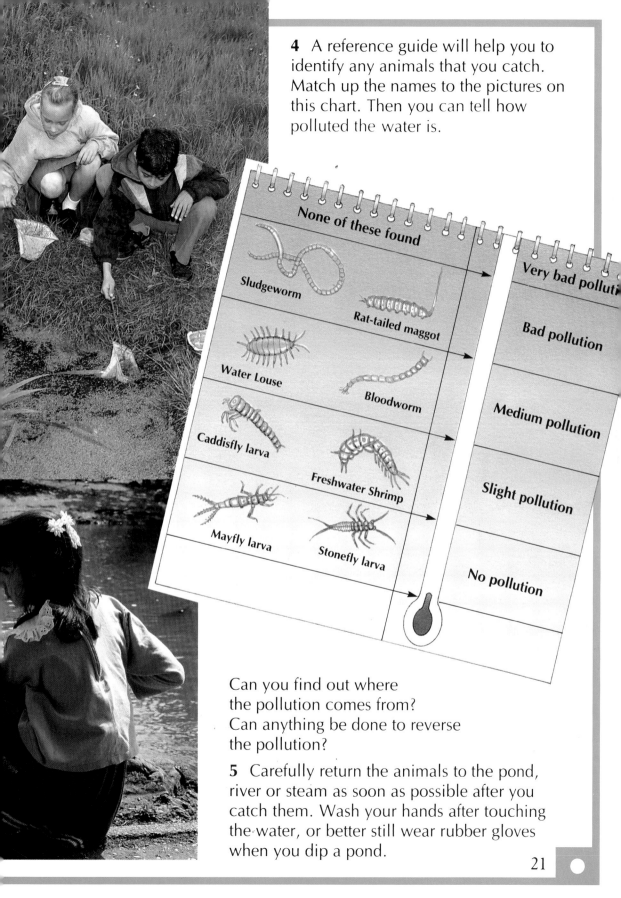

None of these found

Sludgeworm

Rat-tailed maggot

Water Louse

Bloodworm

Caddisfly larva

Freshwater Shrimp

Mayfly larva

Stonefly larva

Very bad polluti

Bad pollution

Medium pollution

Slight pollution

No pollution

Can you find out where the pollution comes from? Can anything be done to reverse the pollution?

5 Carefully return the animals to the pond, river or steam as soon as possible after you catch them. Wash your hands after touching the water, or better still wear rubber gloves when you dip a pond.

21

Unwelcome guests

When people take animals or plants to a new country and allow them to become wild, it can endanger the existing wildlife of that country.

In the late 1800s, Grey Squirrels from North America were released in England and Scotland. Now the Grey Squirrel has spread to most parts of Britain. It has become a pest because it has few natural enemies in Britain, where there was already a smaller Red Squirrel which did very little damage. Grey Squirrels damage trees and rob birds of their eggs and young.

The Cane Toad of South and Central America, one of the world's largest toads, was recently introduced into Australia. It was thought that the Cane Toads would be able to control the number of Cane Beetles, a pest which was destroying the Australian sugar cane crop.

◀ Introduced fish species can also endanger wildlife. In 1960, fish called Nile Perch were put into three large lakes in Africa to provide food for the local people. The Perch ate so many other fish in the lakes that today, a third of the 1000 native species of fish have become extinct.

The plan was a complete disaster. Not only did the Cane Toads fail to keep the numbers of Cane Beetles under control, they spread across Australia, eating the native frogs and toads, small mammals and snakes. The Cane Toad has few predators, because its skin contains a poison and any animal trying to eat it would suffer a painful death.

Habitat destruction

Every kind of animal or plant lives in particular surroundings which it shares with many others. This is its habitat. The habitat provides the animal with food, water, shelter and somewhere to rear its young. When a habitat is destroyed, all or most of its wildlife is destroyed with it.

Wading birds such as this Avocet depend for their survival on marshes and wetlands.

People are destroying habitats all over the world. Marshes and wetlands are being drained to be turned into harbours, or to provide land for farming or for roads, houses and factories.

When these habitats are destroyed, millions of wading birds, which feed on small animals in the mud, can no longer find food. Frogs, toads and newts have nowhere to live or breed. The drainage of coastal marshes affects people too, because it destroys the breeding grounds for fish that are caught in the open sea.

▶ Hedges provide many birds and other animals with places to breed and feed. But in Europe and many other parts of the world, hedgerows have been pulled out to make fields bigger. In Cameroon, a hedgerow construction scheme is helping to replace many of the hedgerows which had been destroyed to make more land available for farming.

The tropical rainforests provide a home for at least two million different kinds of plants and animals. But nearly half of the rainforests in the world have been cut down to supply trees to the timber industry or to make way for farms, mines and cattle ranches.

Over 10% of the Amazon rainforest has been burned down to make way for cattle ranches.

As the forests are cut down, the habitats of millions of animals and plants are destroyed. If the destruction continues at the present rate, the rainforests will have disappeared by the year 2050.

What you can do

* Join a tree-planting group and help to plant trees in your area. Trees provide important wildlife habitats.

* Persuade people not to buy furniture and other products made from tropical hardwoods such as Teak and Mahogany. This will help to save the tropical forests.

* Save and recycle paper. As paper is made from wood, this helps to save tree habitats.

Protecting wildlife

One way to save wildlife is to create national parks and nature reserves. These provide safe places for animals and plants to live and breed.

Sometimes nature reserves are set up to protect one or two rare animals or plants, sometimes they protect a large habitat such as an area of mountain or moorland or sand dunes by the sea.

National parks contain huge, enclosed areas of land where wild animals are protected in their natural habitats. Worldwide, there are more than 1200 national parks that are open to the public.

An Alaskan Brown Bear fishes for salmon in the Katmai National Park in Alaska in the United States.

The world's first was the Yellowstone Park in the United States, which was set up in 1872. Yellowstone covers 8000 square kilometres of mountains and forests. This is an area about the size of Wales. Amongst the animals it provides a habitat for are elk, bison, moose, bears, wolves and pumas.

Park rangers help to protect the habitat of gorillas living in the mountains of Zaire.

Game wardens in the national parks make sure that the visitors do not disturb the animals, leave litter or start fires. In Africa, wardens carry guns to defend themselves against poachers who may try to kill the wardens if they are caught.

It is also part of a game warden's job to keep the herds of animals from straying outside the park and damaging the crops on neighbouring farms.

Wildlife and zoos

Have you visited a zoo lately? People disagree as to whether zoos are a good way of protecting wild animals and educating people about the need for conservation.

BRITISH ZOOS
RETURN
PERE DAVID'S DEER
TO THE
WILD IN CHINA

▲ A British zoo reared this Père David's Deer in captivity and then returned it to its natural habitat in China.

Some people argue that good zoos have saved endangered species of animals from extinction by breeding them in captivity. At least 18 species have been returned to the wild after captive breeding in zoos, including six species which would otherwise have become completely extinct.

Supporters of zoos say that captive breeding has only become necessary because human activity has destroyed or polluted wildlife habitats and hunting has made whole species of wildlife become extinct.

The Brazilian Golden Lion Marmoset, a tiny monkey, nearly became extinct because so much of its rainforest habitat had been destroyed. Zoos began to breed marmosets and release the young into protected areas in Brazil.

Other people think that zoos are unnecessary and can even be damaging to wildlife. They argue that natural history films can show people how animals live in their natural environments and that there is no longer any need to take animals from the wild to keep in zoos.

Some people think that it is cruel to keep animals in cramped, small cages. The animals do not have enough space to roam about and have nothing to do all day, so they cannot behave naturally and instead become bored and stressed.

What do you think about zoos? How would you design a zoo enclosure to provide an animal with space to move about, somewhere quiet to sleep and with plenty of things to hold its interest?

◄ Do you think that animals should be trained to entertain people?

Make a wildlife reserve

Why not make your own wildlife reserve? A garden wildlife reserve is good fun and you can learn a lot by watching the animals that move into it. If you don't have a garden at home, you could encourage your school to start a wildlife reserve in a quiet corner of the school grounds.

Here are some ideas to start you off. Even if you only use one or two of them you will make the area more welcoming to wildlife.

Buddleias are often described as butterfly bushes.

▲ Buddleia and lavender are easy to grow and their flowers attract bees, butterflies and other insects. Honeysuckle bushes attract moths, while birds may build nests in these plants.

◀ Log piles attract crowds of minibeasts and often larger creatures too, such as hedgehogs and toads. Make a small heap of rotting logs in one corner of your wildlife reserve. Cover part of it with dead leaves. You won't have to wait long to see the results!

Stinging nettles are food for the caterpillars of some beautiful butterflies. If you don't want the nettles to spread, plant them in a large pot or bucket.

▶ Build a bird-table and put out bread, bacon scraps, seeds, fruit and nuts for the birds to eat in winter. Remember to provide a supply of fresh clean water for them to drink and bathe in. An upturned dustbin lid makes a good bird-bath.

◀ Make a mini-pond by sinking an old bowl or plastic container into the ground, away from direct sunlight, and filling it with sand, gravel and a few larger stones. Then add water and pond weed. Use pond water if you can; tap water is suitable as long as you let it stand for a few days to let the chlorine disappear.

Remember, wildlife gardeners do not use chemical pesticides and fertilizers. Make a compost heap of your peelings and other rottable waste. Use the compost to help your plants to grow.

31

Useful addresses

If you would like to find out more about the ideas in this book, write to any of these organisations:

British Trust for Conservation Volunteers,
36 St Mary's Street, Wallingford,
Oxfordshire, OX10 0EU.
Conservation Trust,
George Palmer Site, Northumberland Avenue,
Reading, Berkshire, RG1 5AG.
Council for Environmental Education,
School of Education, University of Reading,
London Road, Reading,
Berkshire, RG1 5AG.
Friends of the Earth (UK),
26–28 Underwood Street,
London, N1 7JQ.

Friends of the Earth (Australia),
Chain Reaction Co-operative, P.O. Box 530E,
Melbourne, Victoria 3001.
Friends of the Earth (New Zealand),
P.O. Box 39-065, Auckland West.
Greenpeace (UK),
30–31 Islington Green,
London, N1 8XE.
Greenpeace (Australia),
Studio 14, 37 Nicholson Street,
Balmain, New South Wales 2041.
Greenpeace (New Zealand),
Private Bag, Wellesley Street, Auckland.
People's Trust for Endangered Species,
Hamble House, Meadrow,
Godalming, Surrey, GU7 3JX.
World-Wide Fund for Nature (WWF-UK),
Panda House, Weyside Park,
Godalming, Surrey, GU7 1XR.

Index

acid rain   19
alligators   15
aphids   7

balance of nature   6, 9, 10
birds   16, 22, 24, 25, 30, 31
Blue Whale   4
Brazilian Golden Lion Marmoset   29
breeding grounds   24
bullfrogs   8, 9
butterflies   30, 31

Cane Beetles   23
Cane Toad   23
captive breeding   28
carbon dioxide   6
carnivores   6, 9
caterpillars   31
cheetahs   15
chemicals   19
clothes   10
compost   31
conservation   13
crocodiles   15

deer   16
destroying habitats   24, 25
dinosaurs   12

dolphins   15
drainage   24

eating meat   10
endangered species   13, 15, 28
Europe   8, 16
evolution   12
extinct   12, 13, 15, 16, 23, 28

fertilizers   31
fish   15, 19, 20, 23, 24
food   6–8, 10, 12, 14, 15, 19, 23, 24, 30
food chains   6, 8
food web   6
forest clearance   10, 11
foxes   6, 9
frogs' spawn   17

game wardens   27
gases   19
Grey Squirrel   22

habitats   24–28
herbivores   6, 7
hunting   12, 14, 15, 28

identifying wildlife   5, 21
India   8, 9
insects   8, 17, 20
ivory   14

ladybirds   7, 9
leopards   15
litter   19, 27
lizards   15

magnifying glass   5
mammal   4, 13, 23
marshes   24
medicines   10
moorland   26
mountains   26

national parks   26, 27
naturalist   12
nature reserves   26
Nile Perch   23

ocelots   15
oxygen   10

pests   22, 23
pesticides   19, 31
pets   17
plants   4, 6, 9–14, 18, 22, 25, 26, 30, 31
poachers   14, 27
pollution   15, 18, 20, 21,
pond   17, 20, 21, 31
porpoises   15
predators   9, 23
prey   9
protection of wildlife   13, 28

recycling   25
Red Squirrel   22
reptile   15

scientists   4, 13
sewage   18
shelter   24
snakes   15, 23
species   4, 5, 9, 10, 12, 13, 15, 23, 28
Stone Age   14
sunshine   6

tadpoles   17
tigers   15
tortoises   16
trees   5, 19, 22, 25
tropical rainforests   2?

water   6, 7, 18–21, 24
wetlands   24
wildlife   4, 5, 10, 13, 22–26, 28–31
wildlife reserve   30
wolves   16, 27

zoo   12, 28, 29